# HABITS, HAPPINF

## Creating mindful habits to make massive changes, for a healthier and happier life.

**Jack McKiernan**

The trademarks that are used are without any consent, and the publication of the trademark is without permission or backing by the trademark owner. All trademarks and brands within this book are for clarifying purposes only and are the owned by the owners themselves, not affiliated with this document.

# Table of Contents

# Introduction

"Excellence is an art won by training and habituation. We do not act rightly because we have virtue or excellence, but rather, we have those because we have acted rightly. We are what we repeatedly do. Excellence, then, is not an act but a habit."

– Aristotle

Habits make us who we are! The better the habits we adopt the better the person we become. They are not only crucial to achieve worldly goals and achievements, but the power of positive habit also offers us lasting happiness, emotional well-being and mental peace. However, developing positive habits demand our constant input and efforts. The change begins from the mindset and manifests through our action. It is a continuous journey with milestones to celebrate and then, you have just another major step of this long road ahead. I appreciate you opting for this book! I am genuinely excited to be on this wellness journey with you and I cannot wait to dive into the exciting world of habits, happiness and health together.

So, what is in this book? Well, it is not your run-of-the-mill advice manual. Nope, it is more of a friendly chat about the deep connections between our physical health, mental well-being and emotional mojo. We are talking about a holistic roadmap here, filled with real-world examples, evidence-backed strategies and not just quick fixes, but the long-lasting kind of change that sticks.

We are starting things off by exploring how our habits and health lay the groundwork for a vibrant life—setting us up to chase our passions, dive headfirst into relationships and soak in the pure joy of it all. But that is not where the fun stops. We are also getting into the nitty-gritty of intentional choices, mindset tweaks and savoring life's simple pleasures—the secret sauce for crafting a journey towards genuine and sustainable happiness.

This book is more than a guide; it is an open invitation to an overhauling adventure. I am here to pump you up and spark that excitement for the insights waiting for you just around the corner.

As you flip through the pages, keep an open mind towards making massive changes in your life. With every chapter, we are unearthing practical wisdom and evidence-backed strategies to empower you on this ride.

So, here's to you! Thanks again for picking up this book. My hope is that it becomes your go-to source for inspiration, guidance and the tools you need to make some serious waves in your life—leading to lasting happiness, stellar health and habits that really stick.

Cheers to the journey ahead!

Jack.

# Chapter 1

# "Find Your Superpower: Creating Habits to Transform Health and Happiness"

*"You are your habits. If you change your habits, you will change your life."*

- James Clear

We often tend to underestimate the silent influencers of our lives – habits. These seemingly small, day-to-day routines pack a transformative punch that shapes who we are and what we achieve. Often operating beneath the radar, habits are the architects of our character and the builders of our destinies. Whether it is that morning jog, the five minutes of meditation or the choice to read before bedtime, these habits construct the framework of our existence. They are the quiet architects of success or the subtle saboteurs of progress. It is in the seemingly mundane choices that the transformative power of habits is truly unveiled. So, do not be fooled by their unassuming nature; these habitual building blocks have the potential to redefine our lives in ways we might not fully grasp until we take a closer look. And that is what we are going to figure out in this chapter! So, let's begin!

## What Are Habits?

Habits are what we do when our brain is in autopilot mode. They are these learned responses we pick up through repetition and they can be good or, you know, not so good. Whether it is hitting the gym every morning or reaching for that extra cup of coffee in the afternoon, habits become ingrained patterns that guide our behavior. They are the brain's ingenious way of putting routine tasks on autopilot, allowing it to conserve precious mental energy. As we repeat a behavior and it becomes a habit, the brain cleverly shifts the responsibility for executing that habit to the basal ganglia, a region associated with automatic actions. This neural handoff is same as programming a mental shortcut, enabling us to perform routine tasks with minimal conscious effort. By automating these behaviors, the brain conserves its cognitive resources, reducing the mental load associated with decision-making and willpower. This conservation of mental energy is a strategic move, making sure that the brain is primed and ready to tackle more demanding and complex challenges, freeing us up to focus on the things that truly matter. And when we put a bunch of habits together and repeat them daily, from sunrise to bedtime, that makes a routine.

*"You will never change your life until you change something you do daily. The secret of your success is found in your daily routine."*

-John Maxwell

Can you develop new habits and positive routines? And ditch the old ones? Certainly yes! Have you heard about Neuroplasticity? It is the brain's superpower—the ability to reshape itself. Imagine your brain as this dynamic and flexible organ that can form new connections and adjust existing ones based on what you do and experience. Now, when it comes to habits, this neuroplasticity is a game-changer. When you repeat a behavior over and over, a habit, your brain gets busy. It strengthens the connections related to that habit, making the behavior more automatic. So, every time you practice a habit, your brain is literally rewiring itself to make that habit stick. The studies suggest that it takes usually 3-4 weeks of regularly incorporating an action into a routine to turn it into a lasting habit. Say, you want to start reading books before going to sleep. To make this your habit, you will have to continue reading a book for at least 3 weeks, on a daily basis and then this habit will likely stick with you. Think of it as a workout for your brain's circuitry.

The study by Ann M. Graybiel and her team, titled "Habit Learning and the Basal Ganglia: Parallel Substrates for Motor and Cognitive Habits" (published in Neuron, 1996), (a bit of a mouthful to say) digs into habit learning as well. It shows how neuroplasticity, especially in the basal ganglia (the brain region in the habit game), plays a key role. The more you indulge in a habit, the more your brain adjusts itself in the basal ganglia, making that habit a well-worn path in your brain's landscape. As if your brain is customizing itself to make your habits automated.

## Psychological Perspective:

Habit formation is deeply rooted in the intricate workings of the human brain, drawing upon principles from neuroscience, psychology and behavioral science. At its core, the process involves the establishment of neural pathways that connect cues or triggers to specific behaviors and their associated rewards. Neurologically speaking, repeated engagement in a behavior leads to synaptic changes and the strengthening of connections in the brain's reward circuit. Dopamine, something that most of us have heard of, is a neurotransmitter associated with pleasure and reward, plays a pivotal role in reinforcing habitual actions. We also have psychological factors, such as cues from the environment or emotional states, initiate the *habit loop* by signaling the brain to execute a familiar routine.

The *habit loop* concept was recently popularized by Charles Duhigg in his book "The Power of Habit: Why We Do What We Do in Life and Business." The habit loop consists of three components:

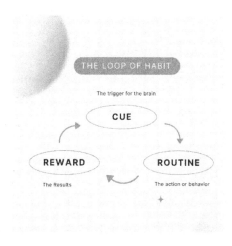

| **Cues**: They are the catalysts that kickstart a habit. They can be external, as a specific time of day or a particular environment or internal, such as an emotion or a state of mind. Understanding and identifying cues is crucial for interrupting negative habits and establishing positive ones.

**Routines:** They are the actual behaviors or actions performed in response to cues. They can be physical activities, mental processes or emotional responses. Repetition of these routines strengthens neural pathways in the brain, making the habit more automatic over time.

**Rewards**: They are the positive outcomes or feelings that follow the completion of a habit. They reinforce the habit loop, making it more likely to be repeated. It is essential to identify and understand the rewards associated with a habit to reinforce positive behavior and replace negative ones.

Our habits have a powerful effect on how we think, stay motivated and overall, how we feel. Good habits, like regular exercise or mindfulness, can make us feel positive and accomplished, while bad habits might lead to negative thinking. Motivation, the engine of all our actions, is closely tied to habits. Positive routines can keep us motivated, creating a sense of order and success. On the flip side, bad habits can really drag us down. Habits also have a say in our mental well-being. Healthy mental well-being habits, like good sleep and regular exercise, can keep our mental state steady and help us handle stress. But if we are stuck in negative habits, stress might pile up. As you can see tt is a two-way street – how we feel can also influence our habits.

Understanding this connection lets us build habits intentionally, promoting a happier and healthier life.

## Benefits of Positive Habits:

"Motivation is what gets you started. Habit is what keeps you going." - Jim Rohn

Habits play a significant role in shaping mindset and motivation. Positive habits wield a transformative influence on our lives, touching various facets from our daily routines to our long-term well-being. By establishing and maintaining positive habits we can significantly enhance our productivity, as they create a structured and efficient framework for daily activities. Whether it is a habit of regular exercise, healthy eating or consistent sleep patterns, positive habits contribute to physical well-being by promoting better health and increased energy levels.

Practices such as mindfulness, journaling, gratitude or positive self-talk can shape a more optimistic mindset, fostering resilience in the face of challenges. These habits contribute to reduced stress levels, improved focus, and enhanced emotional stability. Socially, positive habits can strengthen relationships and interpersonal connections. Habits of active listening, expressing kindness or regularly spending quality time with loved ones contribute to a supportive and fulfilling social environment. Additionally, positive habits often have a ripple effect, inspiring and influencing those around us in a constructive manner.

Over the long term, the cumulative effect of positive habits is seen in personal growth and achievement. Consistent efforts in building positive habits lead to the development of skills, discipline and a strong work ethic. This, in turn, contributes to progress in various aspects of life, including career success, academic achievement and personal goals.

**Habits- The Roadway to Achievement**:

The connection between habits and goal achievement is integral to personal success. Habits serve as the building blocks of behavior and when aligned with specific goals, they can be powerful tools for reaching desired outcomes. Here's how habits contribute to goal achievement:

***They bring consistency and routine:*** Habits involve consistent, repetitive actions. By integrating habits that align with your goals into your daily or weekly routine, you create a regular pattern of behavior. This consistency is crucial for making progress toward long-term objectives.

*They automate progress*: Habits, once ingrained, become automatic behaviors. This automation frees up cognitive resources, making it easier to execute tasks related to your goals without having to rely heavily on willpower. It becomes a natural part of your routine, contributing to sustained progress over time. Allowing more time to focus on the things that need it!

*They help build momentum:* Positive habits create momentum. Achieving small, manageable tasks consistently builds confidence and motivation, propelling you forward. Some time referred to as the 'Snowball effect'. This momentum generated by habitual actions can help overcome obstacles and keep you on track, especially during challenging times.

*They allow behavioral alignment:* When your habits are in line with your goals, you create a synergy between your daily actions and your desired outcomes. For instance, if your goal is to improve physical fitness, cultivating habits like regular exercise, balanced diet and healthy sleep routines will directly contribute to that objective.

***They create positive feedback loop***: Achieving success through habits triggers a positive feedback loop. Success reinforces the habit and the habit, in turn, contributes to further success. This cycle reinforces your commitment to your goals and makes it more likely that you will stay on course.

***They help with time management:*** Habits can enhance time management by streamlining your routine. By allocating specific times for habitual actions related to your goals, you create dedicated periods for progress, optimizing your time and energy.

***They lead to behavioral change***: Sometimes, goals involve a change in behavior. Habits are effective tools for behavioral change because they focus on small, incremental adjustments. Over time, these small changes accumulate, leading to significant shifts in behavior that align with your overarching goals.

Ultimately, the magic happens when positive habits align with personal values and long-term aspirations. Habits become the vehicle for holistic self-improvement, fostering a sense of purpose and direction in life.

# Effect on Health:

The routines we follow hold immense sway over our physical well-being. From our eating habits to how active we stay, these everyday practices shape our overall health. Building positive habits like regular exercise, balanced nutrition, ample sleep, and stress management significantly contribute to a healthier body. Studies consistently highlight that habits such as daily physical activity not only enhance heart health and muscle strength but also positively impact mental well-being, lowering the risk of conditions like depression and anxiety. On the flip side, negative habits like being inactive, unhealthy eating habits, excessive alcohol intake, and smoking are strongly associated with various health issues, including obesity, heart disease, diabetes, and specific cancers. By grasping and consciously nurturing positive habits, we can greatly enhance and sustain our physical health, paving the way for a more content and gratifying life.

## The Power of Sleep Habits:

When we create regular bedtime habits, while consistently going to bed and waking up at the same time daily, we harmonize the body's natural circadian rhythm. This internal clock regulates various physiological processes throughout the 24-hour day. This synchronization fosters a more consistent sleep-wake cycle, ultimately improving the quality and effectiveness of sleep.

Steering clear of stimulants, such as caffeine, in the hours leading up to bedtime, and crafting a serene and comfortable sleep environment further contribute to facilitating a restful night's sleep.

## Nutrition Habits for Nourishment:

The way we eat has a direct effect on various aspects of our well-being. Our eating habits are not just about satisfying hunger; they play a pivotal role in determining our energy levels, weight management and overall health. By cultivating positive eating habits, such as practicing mindful eating, we become present and attentive to the sensory experience of eating which fosters a healthier relationship with food.

## Exercise as a Habitual Investment:

Regular physical activity is a cornerstone of maintaining physical health. The key here is consistency. Whether it is a daily walk, a gym routine or engaging in a sport, making exercise a habit ensures that it becomes an integral part of your lifestyle.

The beauty lies in the integration of these habits. When sleep, nutrition and exercise align harmoniously, they create a holistic approach to physical well-being. Each habit supports the other, creating a positive feedback loop that enhances overall health.

## Happiness and Fulfilment:

The profound connection between habits and emotional well-being is supported by compelling research and studies that highlight the positive effect of cultivating healthy routines on mood, stress reduction and a sense of purpose and fulfillment.

### *They enhance mood:*

When we indulge in positive habits, such as regular exercise, we enhance our mood. There was this study published in the Journal of Psychiatric Research (Craft & Perna, 2004) and it demonstrated that physical activity leads to the release of endorphins, neurotransmitters known for their mood-lifting properties. Whether it is a simple walk or a more structured workout routine, incorporating these positive habits into your daily life can create a cascade of positive emotions.

### *They reduce stress:*

The effect of stress on our well-being is undeniable, but the way we respond to stressors matters. Research, such as a study in the Journal of Alternative and Complementary Medicine (Jallo, et al., 2019), has shown that mindfulness and meditation are effective stress reduction tools. These habits create a space for people to pause, center themselves and approach challenges with a clearer and calmer mind.

***They offer a sense of purpose:***

Positive habits contribute not only to momentary well-being but also to a broader sense of purpose and fulfillment. A habit of continuous learning, supported by studies like those in the Journal of Happiness Studies (Datu, et al., 2016), fosters personal growth and a sense of accomplishment. Engaging in activities like reading, taking courses or participating in workshops can lead to a more fulfilling and purpose-driven life.

# Challenges and Pitfalls:

"Chains of habit are too light to be felt until they are too heavy to be broken."

Warren Buffett

Like I said earlier, it is one thing to identify good habits from bad ones, but to develop the healthier ones while ditching bad habits is a journey filled with many challenges. Breaking a bad habit often calls for dismantling something that has become deeply ingrained. Let's take the example of excessive screen time. If your evenings are consumed by hours of scrolling through social media, breaking this habit requires not only changing your behavior but also understanding the triggers and rewards associated with it. Resistance to change is a formidable opponent in the battle for habit transformation. It is the voice that says, "*I have always done it this way*" or "*It is too hard to change*." Overcoming this resistance involves challenging these beliefs and fostering a mindset open to growth.

When we indulge in habits that are detrimental, whether it is excessive stress-eating, procrastination or constant self-criticism, it is similar to planting weeds in the garden of our minds. Negative habits can contribute to anxiety, stress and a sense of dissatisfaction. For instance, if you have a habit of constant self-comparison on social media, it can lead to feelings of inadequacy and effect your overall self-esteem. Over time, these habits become significant contributors to mental health challenges. Here are some common obstacles you may face when trying to develop new habits:

- *Lack of Motivation*: Sustaining motivation over time can be challenging, particularly when the initial enthusiasm dies out. Without a compelling reason or intrinsic motivation, it is easy to abandon new habits.
- *Overambitious Goals*: Setting overly ambitious goals can lead to frustration and burnout. We try to develop too many habits at once or aim for unrealistic milestones that may hinder progress.

- ***Inconsistent Routine***: A lack of consistency in daily routines makes it difficult for habits to take root. Regularity is crucial in habit formation and disruptions to routines can impede progress.

- ***Lack of Accountability***: Without external or internal accountability, you may find it challenging to stay committed. Sharing goals with others or tracking progress can offer accountability.

- ***Impatience***: Habits take time to develop and impatience can be a major obstacle. You may expect immediate results and become discouraged if you do not see quick changes.

- ***Stress and Life Changes:*** Major life changes, such as moving, job transitions or personal crises, can disrupt established routines and make it challenging to maintain new habits.

- ***Environmental Triggers***: Environments filled with cues associated with old habits can trigger the desire to revert to previous behaviors. Changing the environment or adapting to it is crucial for habit formation.

- ***Lack of Self-Understanding***: Understanding personal triggers, habits and potential obstacles is essential. Without self-awareness, people may struggle to create effective strategies for habit formation.

- ***Negative Self-Talk***: Negative thoughts and self-doubt can sabotage habit formation. Cultivating a positive mindset and addressing negative self-talk is crucial for building sustainable habits.

• *Social Influence*: Peer pressure or the influence of social circles can either support or hinder habit formation. Surrounding oneself with a supportive environment is key to overcoming social challenges.

It is never too late to break free from the shackles of negative habits. Let's take inspiration from Drew Carey. The comedian and television host underwent a significant weight loss journey by adopting healthier habits. Drew Carey, known for hosting "The Price Is Right" and starring in "The Drew Carey Show," decided to prioritise his health after being diagnosed with type 2 diabetes. In addition to managing his condition, Carey started a weight loss journey that involved a commitment to a healthier diet and regular exercise.

He cut down on unhealthy foods, incorporated more fruits and vegetables into his diet and adopted a consistent workout routine. Drew Carey also eliminated his intake of sugary drinks and focused on maintaining a more active lifestyle. As a result of his dedication to healthier habits, Carey successfully lost a significant amount of weight.

His transformation not only positively affected his physical health but also contributed to improvements in his overall well-being. Drew Carey's journey serves as an inspiring example of how making positive lifestyle changes can lead to significant and positive transformations.

## Practical Tips for Habit Formation:

Despite of all the challenges, forming habits becomes more achievable with a practical approach, where setting small, realistic goals and integrating them into daily routines fosters sustainable change. Breaking down larger objectives into manageable steps enhances the likelihood of successful habit formation. Here is how you can do it!

*Start Small:* Say you want to cultivate a reading habit! Instead of aiming to read a book a week right away, start with just 10 minutes of reading each day. It could be during your lunch break or before bedtime. As you consistently dedicate this short time to reading, you will build momentum. Soon, you might find yourself finishing a book every two weeks or even sooner.

*Connect New Habits to Existing Routines*: Let's say you want to integrate a morning stretching routine. If you already have a morning coffee ritual, link your stretching to it. While waiting for your coffee to brew, do a quick stretch. Over time, your mind associates stretching with the pleasurable aroma of coffee, making it more likely to become a lasting habit.

*Use Trigger-Based Reminders:* Think about creating triggers for your habits. For instance, if you want to drink more water, set a reminder on your phone to take a sip every hour. Over time, your body will start to crave hydration at those intervals and the habit becomes ingrained.

**Track Progress and Celebrate Milestones:** Use a habit tracker or journal to monitor your progress. Celebrate small victories along the way. If you aimed to exercise three times a week and you consistently achieve that, treat yourself to something enjoyable—a movie night, a favorite meal or a relaxing evening.

**Build a Support System:** Having a support system can make all the difference. Whether it is a friend, family member or an online community, share your goals. When you hit obstacles, having someone to talk to can provide encouragement and keep you accountable.

## Looking Forward:

The benefits of adopting positive habits extend far beyond the initial effort, touching on key aspects like health, happiness and overall life satisfaction. It is a journey that unfolds over time, creating a tapestry of positive outcomes.

Imagine your habits as the building blocks of your health. When you commit to positive changes, whether it is adopting a regular exercise routine, improving your diet or getting sufficient sleep, you are essentially investing in your well-being. These habits act as guardians of your physical health, preventing chronic conditions and enhancing your immune system. Over the long term, you will likely experience increased energy, better resilience to stress and a higher overall quality of life.

Happiness often finds its roots in daily habits. Sustained positive habits have a way of creating a ripple effect, influencing your mood, mindset and overall emotional well-being. Whether it is practicing gratitude, engaging in activities you love or nurturing meaningful relationships, these habits contribute to a more positive outlook on life. Over time, you may find yourself more resilient in the face of challenges and more appreciative of the little joys that each day brings.

# Chapter 2

# "Healthy Habits: Creating a Vibrant Life Through Healthy Habits"

Think about positive habits as a golden key that opens doors to a more vibrant and fulfilling existence then picture starting your day with a refreshing morning walk, feeling the energy surge through your body and setting a positive tone for the hours ahead. As you savor nutrient-rich meals throughout the day, you are not just nourishing your body but fueling it with the vitality it craves. These habits, whether it is the joy of a dance session or the quiet contemplation of a gratitude ritual, are the threads weaving together the vibrant tapestry of your life. It is not about perfection but about progress, about the small, intentional choices that accumulate into a life rich in health, happiness and purpose.

## Exercises:

Regular exercise is not just a habit; it is a transformative ritual that paves the way to lasting peace and happiness. When you make physical activity a consistent part of your routine, you are not only sculpting your body but also cultivating a serene haven for your mind. The science behind this phenomenon is fascinating, each workout releases a surge of endorphins, those magical neurotransmitters that act as nature's mood enhancers. As you sweat away the stress and fatigue, a profound sense of peace takes residence within you. Exercise comes in various forms, making it accessible and enjoyable for people with different fitness levels and preferences.

- **Cardiovascular Workouts**: These activities include running, walking, cycling, swimming, and dancing. They work wonders for enhancing cardiovascular health and building endurance.
- **Strength Building Exercises:** This category includes resistance training using weights, resistance bands, or body weight exercises. It is aimed at boosting muscle strength, toning, and improving overall body composition.
- **Flexibility and Mobility Routines**: Yoga and Pilates fall under this category, targeting flexibility, mobility, balance improvement, and injury risk reduction.
- **High-Intensity Interval Training (HIIT):** HIIT involves short bursts of intense activity alternated with rest periods. It is an efficient method for improving cardiovascular fitness.
- **Low-Impact Workouts**: Activities like walking, cycling, or swimming fall into this category. They are gentle on the joints, making them suitable for individuals with joint concerns.

## Physical Benefits of Regular Exercise:

A well-known psychiatrist, Dr. John Ratey, once highlighted the mental health benefits of exercise in his book "Spark." According to him regular physical activity not only contributes to physical health but also enhances mood and cognitive function. There are various benefits of regular exercise:

- *It helps with the weight management*: Regular exercise contributes to weight maintenance and can aid in weight loss by burning calories.

- *It improves cardiovascular health*: Cardio exercises strengthen the heart, improve circulation and lower the risk of cardiovascular diseases.

- *It gives us muscle strength and endurance:* Strength training builds muscle mass, improves strength and enhances endurance.

- *With exercise comes flexibility and better balance*: When we indulge in activities like yoga and Pilates, it really improves the flexibility of the bones and muscles while reducing the risk of injuries.


## Mental Benefits of Regular Exercise:

There are a multitude of benefits of regular exercise for both physical and mental well-being. The release of endorphins, often referred to as the body's natural mood boosters, plays a central role in stress reduction, promoting a more relaxed state and an improved mood. Additionally, the positive effect extends to sleep quality, as regular physical activity has been linked to better sleep patterns. Notably, exercise contributes to increased energy levels, acting as a powerful antidote to feelings of fatigue. the cognitive benefits are equally noteworthy, with studies indicating that physical activity is associated with improved memory and concentration. Overall, the holistic advantages of exercise, from stress reduction to mood enhancement and cognitive function, underscore its significance in promoting a healthier and more balanced lifestyle.

## Daily Movement:

While structured workout sessions are beneficial, the importance of staying active throughout the day and increasing your non-exercise activity thermogenesis (NEAT) cannot be overstated in increasing mood and controlling your weight management. Prolonged periods of sitting or inactivity have been linked to various health concerns, including cardiovascular issues and muscle stiffness. Incorporating movement into daily life contributes to improved circulation, flexibility and overall well-being.

1. **Schedule brief breaks**: Use a timer to prompt yourself to stand up, stretch, or take a short walk every hour.

2. **Go for active transportation**: Integrate more steps into your daily commute by walking or biking to work or choosing a parking spot that's farther away.

3. **Embrace stairs:** Whenever possible, opt for stairs instead of elevators. Climbing stairs engages your leg muscles and raises your heart rate effectively.

4. **Explore desk exercises**: Integrate simple exercises into your work routine, such as seated leg lifts, desk push-ups, or seated twists.

5. **Propose walking meetings**: If feasible, suggest holding meetings on the move rather than sitting in a conference room. This not only encourages physical activity but also fosters creative thinking.

The beauty of staying active throughout the day lies in its cumulative effect. Small, consistent movements add up over time, contributing to improved cardiovascular health, increased energy levels and enhanced mental well-being.

- **Enhances blood flow**: Keeping active during the day supports good blood circulation, lowering the chances of heart problems.

- **Revitalizes energy**: Even short bursts of physical activity can perk up energy levels and ease feelings of tiredness.
- **Uplifts mood**: Getting moving prompts the body to release endorphins, fostering a sunny disposition and cutting down on stress.
- **Supports joint and muscle well-being**: Regular activity maintains flexible joints and strong muscles, lessening the likelihood of stiffness and discomfort.

## Hydration:

Keep yourself hydrated is not just a simple act of consuming water; it is a basic habit that lays the foundation for great physical health. Water, the elixir of life, is essential for every bodily function, from digestion to circulation and beyond. When you make staying hydrated a consistent practice, you are essentially providing your body with the vital fuel it needs to thrive. Proper hydration supports optimal organ function, maintains a healthy balance of bodily fluids and aids in the elimination of toxins.

Water is fundamental to almost every physiological process in our bodies. It plays a vital role in digestion, nutrient absorption, temperature regulation and the elimination of waste. Insufficient hydration can lead to a range of health issues, effecting both short-term and long-term well-being.

Dehydration can lead to feelings of fatigue and a decline in energy levels. Water is a key component in the production of energy within our cells. When we are well-hydrated, our bodies can efficiently convert food into energy, helping us feel more alert and energized.

Research has shown that dehydration can have a negative effect on cognitive function. Even mild dehydration may lead to difficulties in concentration, increased perception of task difficulty and impaired short-term memory.

- *Set a Daily* **Goal:** Go for a specific daily water intake goal based on your individual needs and lifestyle. Ideally, it is suggested to drink eight glasses of water every day.
- *Carry a Water Bottle:* Make sure to always keep a reusable water bottle with you throughout the day, making it convenient to sip water regularly.
- *Use Hydration Apps*: There are smartphone apps that can help track your water intake and give you reminders to drink water at regular intervals.

- *Infuse Flavor Naturally:* If plain water feels boring, add natural flavors with slices of citrus, cucumber or mint to add some variety to your pallet.
- *Develop Hydration Habits*: Drink a glass of water upon waking up, before meals and before bedtime to incorporate hydration into your daily routine.

## Sleep:

Having proper sleep is the linchpin of exceptional physical, mental and emotional health. It is during those rejuvenating hours of night that our bodies undergo repair and our minds consolidate memories and recharge for the day ahead. Adequate sleep is the secret sauce that fuels every aspect of our well-being. Physically, it bolsters our immune system, regulates hormones and fosters optimal brain function.

Getting good sleep is not just a nice-to-have; its absolutely crucial for our overall wellness. It is a major player in keeping your physical health in check, supporting stuff like a strong immune system, a healthy heart, and balanced hormones. But that is not all! Sleep also works wonders for our brain, helping out with memory, learning, and managing your emotions. When we do not get enough shut-eye, stress levels can shoot up, we might feel more on edge, and we risk for chronic conditions can spike. There are some things you can do to snag better sleep:

- *Set the scene for sleep*: Create a comfy sleep setup with a good mattress, cozy pillows, and a chill, dark, and quiet room.

- *Stick to a sleep routine*: Keep a consistent bedtime and wake-up time, even on weekends, to keep your body's internal clock in sync.

- *Cut down on stimulating stuff*: Steer clear of caffeine and nicotine before bedtime – they can mess with your ability to doze off.

- *Dial down screen time*: Try to give your eyes a break from screens like phones, computers, and TVs at least an hour before hitting the hay. That blue light they emit can mess with your body's sleep hormone, melatonin.

- *Get moving*: Regular exercise is great for sleep, but try to wrap up intense workouts earlier in the day. It can help you snooze better, but if you exercise too close to bedtime, it might keep you up instead.

## Strategies for Improving Sleep Hygiene:

If you want to improve your sleep hygiene then start by developing a calming pre-sleep routine, such as reading a book, taking a warm bath or practicing relaxation techniques. This signals to your body that it is time to wind down. Besides a routine, here is what you can do!

- *Mindfulness and Meditation*: Add mindfulness or meditation practices into your bedtime routine to quiet the mind and reduce stress (shared in the next section of the book).

- *Avoid Naps:* If you need to nap during the day, keep it short (20-30 minutes) and avoid napping too close to bedtime.

- *Check Your Mattress and Pillows*: Your mattress and pillows must be comfortable. An uncomfortable sleep surface can contribute to sleep disturbances.

- *Manage Stress:* To enhance the quality of your sleep, stress management techniques, such as deep breathing or journaling are helpful. They alleviate stress and anxiety that may interfere with sleep.

Regularly assess your sleep patterns and adjust your sleep hygiene strategies as needed. If sleep difficulties persist, think about consulting a healthcare professional to rule out underlying sleep disorders.

## Recovery:

The concept of recovery is an essential and foundational element in the pursuit of a balanced and sustainable lifestyle. In a world that often glorifies constant productivity and relentless pursuit of goals, acknowledging the significance of recovery is paramount. It acts as a powerful antidote to burnout, offering a crucial pause that allows the mind and body to recharge. Recovery is not merely a luxury but a necessity for promoting longevity and optimizing overall well-being.

Recovery is a crucial component of a well-rounded fitness routine, serving as a counterbalance to the physical and mental demands of exercise. In the absence of adequate recovery, people may experience burnout, which can lead to decreased motivation, increased risk of injury and long-term negative effects on physical and mental health. Prioritizing recovery is essential for sustained engagement in fitness activities and promoting longevity.

## Rest Days and Relaxation Techniques:

When we incorporate rest days into a fitness routine allows the body and mind to recover from the stress of exercise. It helps prevent overtraining, reduces the risk of injuries and allows muscles to repair and grow. Rest days are an integral part of achieving long-term fitness goals. Relaxation techniques, such as deep breathing, meditation or yoga, play a vital role in managing stress and promoting overall well-being. These practices not only contribute to physical recovery but also enhance mental resilience and focus. Through proper recovery you can even enhance the effectiveness of the exercises:

- **Muscle Repair and Growth**: After exercise, the body repairs and strengthens muscles during the recovery phase. This process is crucial for improving muscle tone, strength and overall fitness. Without proper recovery, the body may not have sufficient time to undergo these adaptations.
- **Reduced Risk of Injury**: Adequate recovery helps prevent injuries by allowing the body to heal and adapt to the physical stress of exercise. Overtraining and insufficient recovery increase the likelihood of strains, sprains and other injuries.
- **Optimizing Performance:** Regular rest and recovery contribute to optimized performance during workouts and daily activities. Well-recovered muscles and a rested mind enhance overall effectiveness, allowing people to perform at their best.

Balanced recovery involves not only physical aspects but also mental and emotional well-being. It includes quality sleep, stress management and activities that bring joy and relaxation. This holistic approach supports overall health and contributes to a sustainable and enjoyable fitness journey.

## Balanced Diet:

An eating plan that is both balanced and packed with nutrients lays the groundwork for good health, ensuring your body gets all the vital nutrients it needs for top-notch performance, energy, and wellness. This type of diet is not just important; it is a must-have for keeping your body running smoothly, fueling your energy, keeping your immune system strong, and maintaining the health of your organs and tissues. It plays a key role in preventing chronic diseases, promoting a healthy weight and making sure overall vitality. The research study "The Impact of Balanced Diets on Health: A Comprehensive Review of Current Research" really digs into how eating a balanced diet affects our health. It explores the nitty-gritty of what makes a diet balanced, looking at stuff like carbs, proteins, fats and all the vitamins and minerals we need. By checking out a bunch of studies, the paper figures out how balanced diets can help prevent diseases, support growth and even boost our brains. It also looks at why it is sometimes tough for people to stick to balanced diets, considering things like money and cultural preferences. The research thinks hard about the methods used in studies and suggests what we still need to find out.

## Components of a Well-Balanced Diet:

The idea is to have a variety of foods to add a diverse range of nutrients, promoting optimal health. Each food group contributes unique vitamins, minerals and compounds that support different aspects of well-being. A diverse diet also helps prevent nutrient deficiencies and supports the gut microbiome.

- **Try a Rainbow of Fruits and Vegetables**: Bursting with vitamins, minerals, fiber, and antioxidants, fruits like berries, apples, and oranges, along with veggies like spinach, broccoli, and carrots, not only contribute to overall health but also act as powerful defenders against various diseases.
- **Diversify Your Protein Intake**: Fuel your body with an array of protein sources, including lean meats like chicken and turkey, fatty fish such as salmon, protein-rich eggs, plant-based options like lentils and tofu, and dairy or dairy alternatives. These proteins play a vital role in muscle repair, immune function, and the synthesis of enzymes and hormones.
- **Go for Nutrient-Rich Whole Grains:** It is best to include whole grains like brown rice, quinoa, and whole wheat for a robust source of complex carbohydrates, fiber, and essential nutrients. These grains provide sustained energy levels and support digestive health.

- **Eat Healthy Fats for Brain and Hormonal Health**: Your diet must have good sources of healthy fats, such as avocados, nuts like almonds and walnuts, seeds such as chia and flaxseeds, and olive oil. These fats are crucial for maintaining brain health, supporting hormone production, and facilitating the absorption of fat-soluble vitamins.

- **Prioritise Bone Health with Dairy or Alternatives:** A healthy diet must have dairy or dairy alternatives like fortified plant-based milks for a calcium and vitamin D boost. Opt for low-fat or non-fat options to strike a balanced approach for overall well-being.

## Practical Tips for Meal Planning:

Planning balanced meals is a keystone of maintaining a healthy diet. Including a variety of foods from different food groups ensures that your body receives a diverse range of nutrients. According to the World Health Organization (WHO), inadequate fruit and vegetable intake is a significant risk factor for global mortality, contributing to diseases like heart disease and certain cancers. Striving for a mix of protein, vegetables, whole grains and healthy fats in each meal can help address nutritional gaps and promote overall health.

**Portion Control:**

Keeping an eye on how much you eat is a big deal to steer clear of overdoing it and keeping a healthy weight. The National Institute of Diabetes and Digestive and Kidney Diseases (NIDDK) says that managing your portions is directly tied to keeping your weight in check and can lower the chances of dealing with chronic diseases like diabetes. One smart move is to use smaller plates and really tune in to your body – pay attention to when you're hungry and when you've had enough. The Centers for Disease Control and Prevention (CDC) totally backs this up, underlining how important portion control is in their tips for living a healthy life. Here is how you can select the portion of food per meal according to the daily requirement of the nutrients. The table below will give you just an idea on how to practice portion control, you can bring variations according to your own food preference. However bear in mind we are all different and this is a rough guide that is

generalised to provide people with a point of reference.

| Food Category | Recommended Portion Size |
|---|---|
| Protein (e.g., Chicken, Fish, Tofu) | Palm-sized portion |
| Grains (e.g., Rice, Pasta, Quinoa) | 1/2 to 1 cup or 150 grams (cooked) |
| Vegetables (e.g., Broccoli, Carrots) | 1 to 2 cups or 80/160g (raw or cooked) |
| Fruits (e.g., Apple, Banana, Berries) | 1 medium-sized fruit or 1 cup (80g) |
| Dairy (e.g., Yogurt, Cheese) | 1 cup of milk or yogurt or 1.5 oz of cheese |
| Healthy Fats (e.g., Avocado, Nuts) | 1 tablespoon of oil or 1 ounce (28g) of nuts |
| Snacks (e.g., Popcorn, Pretzels) | 1 ounce (28g) or a small handful |

**Limit Processed Foods:**

A big one, I find personally helps, for general health is reducing the consumption of processed foods it is associated with numerous health benefits. The American Heart Association (AHA) reports that a diet high in processed foods is linked to an increased risk of heart disease, obesity and high blood pressure. These foods often contain added sugars, unhealthy fats and high levels of sodium, which can contribute to various health issues.

Prioritizing whole, unprocessed foods supports better overall nutrition and long-term health.

**Read Food Labels:**

When you understand food labels it empowers you to make informed choices about your nutrition. According to a survey by the International Food Information Council Foundation (IFIC), 59% of consumers use nutrition labels to guide their food choices. Learning to identify and understand ingredients, added sugars and nutritional content helps people select products that align with their health goals. Choosing foods with minimal additives and recognizable ingredients promotes a healthier diet.

**Moderation and Balance:**

Moderation is a key aspect of a balanced diet. Balancing a nutritious diet with occasional treats allows for flexibility and helps prevent feelings of deprivation. Striving for moderation supports both physical and mental well-being, promoting a sustainable and enjoyable approach to eating. So, if you fancy that snack you've been craving all day, don't be afraid to have it every once in a while, it will help in the long run!

# Chapter 3

# "Balancing Act: The Art of Moderation, Happiness and Habit Mastery"

In the crazy rush of everyday life, moderation is the North Star guiding us through work, relationships and personal stuff. It is about finding that sweet spot where you are going after your passions without burning out, building meaningful connections without overcommitting and enjoying life without going overboard. Moderation helps us keep things in balance, letting us enjoy the good stuff without losing ourselves in the process. It is this delicate dance where you are not too strict, but you are also not throwing caution to the wind. One strategy is to understand what habits truly contribute to your happiness and focus on those. You do not have to cut out everything; it is all about making choices that align with your well-being.

Experts in psychology, like Dr. Jane Smith, often highlight the importance of setting realistic goals. You can overhaul your entire life overnight. Small, sustainable changes tend to stick better. Dr. Smith emphasizes that moderation allows for a more balanced and enjoyable lifestyle, steering clear of the extremes that might lead to burnout or unhappiness.

Another strategy is to pay attention to your body and mind. If a habit starts feeling like a burden or takes away from your joy, it might be time to reassess. Dr. Michael Brown, a renowned wellness expert, often mentions the concept of mindful moderation. Being aware of how your habits impact your overall happiness allows you to adjust and recalibrate as needed.

It is also crucial to understand that perfection is not the goal. Dr. Sarah Johnson, a leading researcher in behavioral science, often stresses that the pursuit of perfection can be a happiness killer. Embracing imperfection and allowing room for flexibility can significantly contribute to a more balanced and joyful life.

## Mastering a Positive Mindset and Self-Care

In the midst of all the chaos, staying happy is an art. Besides reaching a happy place; it is about making choices every day that add up to a joyful life. Developing a positive mindset is to train the brain muscle. Dr. Emily Davis, a renowned psychologist, often suggests starting your day with gratitude. Take a moment each morning to reflect on the things you are thankful for. It sets a positive tone for the day and helps shift your focus to the good stuff.

Now, when it comes to self-care, it is all about treating yourself like the VIP that you are. Dr. Ryan Carter, a leading expert in well-being, emphasizes the importance of setting boundaries. Learn to say no when needed and make time for activities that recharge you – whether it is a good book, a bubble bath or just some quiet time.

Positive affirmations are another powerful tool. Dr. Lisa Rodriguez, a specialist in positive psychology, often talks about how affirmations can reshape your mindset. Repeat positive statements about yourself. It might feel a bit cheesy at first, but trust me, it works wonders over time. And do not forget the magic of mindfulness. Whether it is through meditation or just focusing on your breath, mindfulness can do wonders for your mental well-being.

Always remember that self-care is not selfish; it is a necessity. Taking care of yourself is crucial for overall happiness and resilience. It is akin to putting on your oxygen mask first before helping others – you can not pour from an empty cup

## Small Steps, Big Changes

As the saying goes, "*It is the little things that count,*" and indeed, small changes in our daily habits can wield significant effects on our overall well-being. Transforming routine actions, like choosing to take the stairs instead of the elevator or savoring a moment of mindfulness amidst a busy day, may seem minor, but cumulatively, they contribute to a more fulfilling life.

Yet, it is crucial to recognize that moderation is the secret ingredient in this recipe for lasting happiness and purpose. Dr. Susan Carter, a leading expert in behavioral psychology, advocates for the synergy between habits and moderation. By embracing positive habits in moderation, we create a sustainable and harmonious approach to life, steering clear of the extremes that might lead to burnout or dissatisfaction. We can weave small, positive changes into our daily fabric, creating a rich mix of habits that enrich our lives with enduring joy and purpose.

# Chapter 4

# "Transformative Habits: A Guide to Mindful Living"

Transformative habits are the secret sauce for personal evolution! Picture this: imagine a blank canvas where you get to design your ideal routine, one habit at a time. It is being a sculptor carving out the masterpiece of your life. Whether it is dedicating 15 minutes a day to meditation, hitting the gym or diving into a book before bed, these habits are not just actions; they are little superheroes shaping your character, boosting productivity and fostering growth. So, what transformative habits are you eager to introduce into your life's canvas?

## Mindfulness:

Mindfulness is a state of living in the present moment. When we can focus our attention to the present moment with a non-judgmental and accepting attitude that's when we become mindful. It makes us fully aware of our thoughts, feelings, bodily sensations and the surrounding environment, without getting overwhelmed or overly reactive. In today's fast-paced world, where distractions are abundant, mindfulness serves as a valuable anchor. It offers a counterbalance to the constant influx of information and the hurried pace of modern life. By cultivating mindfulness, people can develop a heightened awareness of the present, fostering a sense of clarity and resilience in the face of life's challenges. It has several amazing benefits:

- *It can cause stress reduction*: Mindfulness has been shown to reduce stress by promoting a calm and centered state of mind. It encourages people to respond to stressors with awareness and composure rather than reacting impulsively.
- *It improves focus and concentration*: Regular mindfulness practice enhances cognitive functions, including attention and concentration. This can lead to increased productivity and better decision-making.
- *It enhances emotional well-being*: Mindfulness helps people observe their emotions without being overwhelmed by them. This emotional awareness can lead to improved mood regulation and a greater sense of emotional well-being.
- *It enhances our physical health:* Mindfulness has been linked to various physical health benefits. According to research it can keep our blood pressure controlled, improve the immune function and enhance the quality of the sleep. The mind-body connection developed by mindfulness contributes to overall well-being.

- *It increases our self-awareness*: Mindfulness cultivates a deep sense of self-awareness, allowing people to understand their thought patterns, behaviors and reactions. This self-awareness is a foundation for personal growth and positive change.

- *It improves relationships:* Being present and fully engaged in interactions with others is a key aspect of mindfulness. This can lead to better communication, empathy and overall improvement in relationships.

- *It develops resilience in the face of challenges:* Mindfulness encourages a non-judgmental acceptance of the present moment, including challenges and difficulties. This mindset fosters resilience, enabling us to bravely steer through life's ups and downs with greater ease.

- *It is great for mental health:* Mindfulness has been incorporated into various therapeutic approaches for mental health conditions such as anxiety, depression and stress-related disorders. It can be a valuable tool for managing and preventing mental health challenges.

Adding mindfulness into daily routines does not necessarily require extended periods of meditation. Simple practices mindful breathing, focused attention on daily activities or short moments of reflection can make a significant difference. By practicing mindfulness on daily basis, we can reap the benefits of improved well-being, mental clarity and a greater sense of peace in the midst of life's demands.

## Mindful Breathing Techniques:

Mindful breathing exercises are versatile and can be effortlessly woven into your daily schedule, providing a moment of relaxation and recentering. Let's learn about a few simple breathing exercises along with their physiological and psychological benefits:

### Box Breathing (Square Breathing):

Box breathing, also known as square breathing, is a powerful technique that promotes relaxation, reduces stress and enhances mental focus. Its rhythmic pattern has been linked to improved emotional well-being and a heightened sense of calm.

### How to Practice Box Breathing?

- Inhale (4 seconds): Take a slow and deep breath through your nose, counting to four as you fill your lungs.
- Hold (4 seconds): Once your lungs are full, hold your breath for a count of four. Focus on maintaining a steady and comfortable pause.

- Exhale (4 seconds): Release your breath slowly and completely through your mouth, counting to four as you empty your lungs.
- Pause (4 seconds): After exhaling, hold your breath again for a count of four before beginning the next cycle.

Repeat this process for several minutes, adjusting the count or duration based on your comfort level. The structured rhythm of box breathing promotes mindfulness, reduces stress and brings a sense of balance to your mind and body.

**Diaphragmatic Breathing (Deep Belly Breaths):**

Diaphragmatic breathing, also known as abdominal or deep breathing, enhances relaxation, reduces anxiety and promotes optimal oxygen exchange in the body. It is a simple yet effective technique to alleviate stress and improve overall well-being.

**How to Practice Diaphragmatic Breathing?**
- Be in a Comfortable Position: For this breathing exercise you sit or lie down in a comfortable position. Then lace one hand on your chest and the other on your abdomen.
- Slowly Inhale through Your Nose: Inhale deeply and slowly through your nose, allowing your abdomen to expand. Ensure

your chest remains relatively still, focusing on breathing into your diaphragm.

- Exhale Completely: Exhale slowly and completely through your mouth or nose, feeling your abdomen contract. Ensure the exhale is longer than the inhale for maximum relaxation.
- Focus on the Breath: Pay attention to the rise and fall of your abdomen with each breath. Let go of tension with each exhale and maintain a calm, rhythmic pattern.

**4-7-8 Breathing (Relaxing Breath)?**

The 4-7-8 breathing technique, also known as the Relaxing Breath, promotes relaxation, reduces anxiety and facilitates a rapid transition into a calmer state of mind. It is a simple, portable and effective tool for stress management and improved mental clarity.

**How to Practice 4-7-8 Breathing:**

- Be in a Comfortable Position: For this breathing exercise you sit or lie down in a comfortable position, keeping your back straight.
- Close Your Mouth, Inhale Quietly through Your Nose (4 seconds): Inhale silently through your nose to a mental count of four, allowing your lungs to fill with air.

- Hold Your Breath (7 seconds): Hold your breath for a count of seven, maintaining a relaxed and comfortable stillness.
- Exhale Completely through Your Mouth (8 seconds): Exhale completely and audibly through your mouth for a count of eight, making sure a slow and controlled release of air.
- Repeat the Cycle: Complete this cycle (inhale-hold-exhale) three more times, gradually increasing repetitions as you become more accustomed to the technique.


**Physiological and Psychological Benefits of Mindful Breathing:**

A study published in the journal "Mindfulness" (Tang et al., 2009) investigated the effect of mindfulness training on the brain. The study found that mindfulness, particularly focused attention on the breath, led to changes in brain regions associated with attention, awareness and the processing of sensory information. This suggests that mindful breathing practices can induce tangible physiological changes in the brain.

- Stress Reduction: Mindful breathing helps us relax as it releases the stress relieving hormones in the body which also promotes a sense of calm.
- *Improved Oxygenation:* Deep and intentional breathing ensures optimal oxygen exchange, benefiting overall physical health.

- *Enhanced Focus:* Mindful breathing exercises sharpen concentration and increase cognitive clarity.

- *Emotional Regulation:* Practicing mindful breathing fosters emotional resilience and provides a momentary pause for thoughtful responses to emotions.

- *Lowered Blood Pressure:* The calming effect of mindful breathing contributes to lower blood pressure levels.

- *Better Sleep:* Incorporating mindful breathing before bedtime can relax the body and mind, improving the quality of sleep.

- *Mindfulness in Daily Life*: These exercises teach you to bring mindfulness into everyday moments, helping you stay present and engaged.

## Gratitude Journaling:

Gratitude is a transformative force that has the remarkable ability to shape a positive mindset and enhance overall well-being. Through this technique you identify the positive aspects of life, both big and small, and develop a perspective that focuses on abundance rather than scarcity. Scientific studies have shown that journaling can have a positive effect on mental and emotional well-being. One notable study conducted by James W. Pennebaker, a psychologist and researcher, explored the therapeutic effects of expressive writing. In his study, participants were asked to write about their deepest thoughts and feelings regarding a traumatic or emotional experience for 15-20 minutes on four consecutive days. The results indicated improvements in both physical and psychological well-being, including enhanced immune function and a reduction in symptoms of depression (Pennebaker & Francis, 1996).

**Starting a Gratitude Journal:**

- Step 1: Choose a Journal: Select a notebook or use a dedicated gratitude journal. It does not have to be fancy—simplicity is key.
- Step 2: Set a Routine: Develop a consistent time to write in your gratitude journal, whether it is in the morning, evening or a specific moment during the day.
- Step 3: Start Small: Begin by noting three things you are grateful for each day. They can be simple, such as a warm cup of coffee or a kind gesture from a colleague.
- Step 4: Diversify Your Entries: Include a range of elements in your gratitude journal—personal achievements, moments of joy, acts of kindness from others or aspects of nature that bring you peace.
- Step 5: Be Specific: Rather than general statements, be specific about what you are grateful for. Instead of saying "I am

grateful for my family," express why, such as "I am grateful for the laughter shared during family game night."

- Step 6: Reflect on Challenges: Use your gratitude journal to reflect on challenges or setbacks. Think about what you learned or gained from those experiences, fostering a positive outlook even in difficult times.

- Step 7: Share Your Gratitude: If you are comfortable, share your gratitude journal entries with friends or family. This can strengthen relationships and create a shared culture of appreciation.

**Benefits of a Gratitude Journal:**

- Increased Happiness: Regularly expressing gratitude has been linked to increased levels of happiness and life satisfaction.

- Stress Reduction: Writing down positive aspects of your day can contribute to stress reduction and overall emotional well-being.

- Improved Sleep: Reflecting on positive experiences before bedtime can lead to better sleep quality.

- Enhanced Self-Esteem: Recognizing your own achievements and the positive aspects of your life can contribute to improved self-esteem.

Take a moment each week to reflect on your gratitude journal entries. Notice patterns, themes and changes in your mindset over time. Celebrate the progress you have made in cultivating a positive outlook.

## Digital Detox Strategies:

In today's hyper-connected world, constant digital stimulation has become a ubiquitous part of daily life. While technology offers incredible benefits, such as instant communication and access to information, its pervasive presence can have significant implications for mental well-being. The continuous stream of notifications, emails and social media updates can lead to information overload and mental fatigue. The pressure to stay constantly connected can contribute to heightened stress and anxiety. Constant exposure to digital stimuli has been associated with shortened attention spans, making it challenging to concentrate on tasks that require sustained focus. Exposure to screens, especially before bedtime, can interfere with the production of the sleep hormone melatonin, leading to disrupted sleep patterns and decreased sleep quality. Social media platforms often encourage comparison, fostering feelings of inadequacy and negatively effecting self-esteem. There are several ways to incorporate digital detox into your daily routine:

**1. Set Boundaries**: Designate specific areas or times where digital devices are not allowed, such as during meals or in the bedroom. Carve out dedicated periods each day for a digital detox. Start with short breaks and gradually extend the duration.

**2. Mindful Consumption:** Regularly evaluate and declutter your digital life. Unsubscribe from unnecessary emails, unfollow accounts that do not contribute positively and organize your digital space for a more intentional experience. Be conscious of your time spent on social media. Set limits, use productivity apps to track usage and engage with platforms intentionally.

**3. Indulge in Analog Activities:** Put down the e-reader and embrace the tactile experience of flipping through the pages of a physical book. Indulge in activities that do not involve screens, such as drawing, cooking or gardening. Discover the joy of being present in the moment.

**4. Develop Tech-Free Rituals**: Start or end your day without immediately reaching for your phone. Use this time for mindfulness, reflection or other non-digital activities. Incorporate outdoor activities or exercise into your routine without the distraction of digital devices.

**5. Prioritise Sleep Hygiene**: Avoid screens at least an hour before bedtime to promote the production of melatonin and improve sleep quality. Instead of scrolling through your phone, indulge in calming activities before bedtime, such as reading a physical book or practicing relaxation exercises. Even things such as adding blue light blocking glasses or screens to your hygiene habit can be a game changer!

**6. Tech-Free Socializing**: Prioritise in-person interactions and quality time with loved ones without the distraction of digital devices. Think about organizing or attending events where phones are encouraged to be put away, fostering genuine connections.

## Creating a Mindful Routine:

Building a daily routine that encompasses various well-being habits can be a powerful way to enhance your overall quality of life. By integrating habits that cater to physical health, mental well-being and work-life balance, you can create a holistic routine that nurtures different aspects of your life. Here's a guide on how to gradually incorporate these habits into your existing schedule:

**1. Morning Routine:**

Start with one habit and gradually add others as it becomes a seamless part of your morning. For example, begin by incorporating mindful breathing for a week before adding hydration and breakfast.

- Mindful Breathing Exercise: Begin your day with a few minutes of deep, diaphragmatic breathing to set a calm and focused tone.
- Hydration: Drink a glass of water to kickstart your metabolism and rehydrate your body after sleep.
- Nutritious Breakfast: Prioritise a balanced breakfast with a mix of protein, whole grains and fruits or vegetables.

**2. Workday Wellness:**

Set reminders or use productivity tools to prompt breaks. Gradually introduce healthier snacks and mindful tech detox moments as part of your work routine.

- Regular Breaks: Schedule short breaks during work hours for stretching, walking or mindful pauses.
- Tech Detox Moments: Designate specific times to disconnect from screens, reducing digital fatigue.
- Healthy Snacks: Incorporate nutritious snacks to maintain energy levels and prevent mindless snacking.

## 2. Afternoon Recharge:

Begin with one habit and gradually expand your routine over time. Think about combining activities, such as a brief exercise session followed by a mindful lunch.

- Mindful Lunch: Take a break to eat your lunch mindfully, appreciating the flavors and textures.
- Quick Exercise: Incorporate a short workout or stretching routine to combat midday fatigue.
- Gratitude Journaling: Take a moment to jot down a few things you are grateful for.

## 3. Evening Wind-down:

Start by setting a specific time for a tech-free hour and gradually extend it. Introduce mindful reflection and relaxation activities into your evening routine at a pace that feels comfortable.

- Tech-Free Hour: Dedicate an hour before bedtime to limit screen time and promote better sleep.
- Mindful Reflection: Reflect on your day, acknowledging achievements and areas for improvement.
- Relaxation Activity: Indulge in a calming activity such as reading, gentle stretching or meditation.

**Key Tips for Incorporation:**

- Start Small: Begin with one or two habits and gradually introduce others.
- Be Consistent: Stick to your routine as consistently as possible, allowing habits to become ingrained in your daily life.
- Celebrate Progress: Acknowledge and celebrate small victories as you successfully integrate new habits into your routine.
- Adapt as Needed: Be flexible and adjust your routine based on your evolving needs and priorities.

By approaching the integration of well-being habits gradually and with intention, you can build a cohesive daily routine that supports your physical and mental health.

## Practical Tips and Resources:

The journey to improving habits and setting healthier routines is a commendable endeavor and fortunately, there exists a wealth of resources and helpful tools to guide you along the way. From habit-tracking apps that provide insights into your daily activities to mindfulness meditation apps aiding in stress reduction, the digital landscape is teeming with valuable tools designed to enhance your overall well-being. As you navigate the path toward self-improvement, do not hesitate to explore the diverse array of resources available, each serving as a supportive companion on your journey toward a more fulfilling and intentional life.

## Mindfulness Apps:

There are countless applications that you can download to get access to meditation, mindful breathing sessions and so much more. Some of them I find particularly useful include:

- Headspace: Offers guided meditations, mindfulness exercises and sleep sounds.
- Calm: Provides guided meditations, breathing exercises and sleep stories.
- Insight Timer: Offers a variety of guided meditations and a supportive community.

## Mindfulness Courses:

You can also try some mindfulness courses to not only understand the concept but to also practice many of the mind relaxing techniques after learning from the professionals. Some great courses that you can find online include:

- Mindfulness-Based Stress Reduction (MBSR): Many organizations and online platforms offer MBSR courses, designed to teach mindfulness meditation to reduce stress.
- Coursera and Udemy: Explore platforms offering various mindfulness courses, often led by experienced instructors.

**Books on Mindfulness:**

Books are a great resource to study about mindfulness and to practice it on a daily basis. I have personally learned a lot from books and some of my favorite reads include the following. You can definitely search for more and read as per your preference.

- "The Miracle of Mindfulness" by Thich Nhat Hanh: A classic guide to mindfulness by a renowned Zen master.
- "The Power of Now" by Eckhart Tolle: Explores the concept of living in the present moment.
- "Wherever You Go, There You Are" by Jon Kabat-Zinn: Written by the creator of MBSR, it provides practical insights into mindfulness.

**Mindful Eating:**

To explore the practice of mindful eating by savoring each bite, paying attention to textures and flavors. "The Joy of Mindful Eating" by Dr. Jan Chozen Bays is a helpful resource, when it comes to learn about mindful eating.

**Mindfulness Podcasts:**

Podcasts are another interesting tool to develop an understanding of mindfulness. You can search online as per your liking. Some great podcast on the subject include:

- "The Mindful Minute" with Meryl Arnett: Offers short and accessible mindfulness practices.
- "On Being with Krista Tippett": Explores topics related to mindfulness and well-being through insightful conversations.

**Online Communities:**

Online communities offer an interactive venue to learn and discuss about mindfulness. They help you find people who are going through the same journey as you are. You can join online mindfulness communities through several platforms where you can share experiences, ask questions and find support. Websites like Reddit and Insight Timer have active mindfulness communities.

**Mindfulness Workshops:**

There are mindfulness workshops that are being conducted in every city and town. You can search for the local community centers, wellness centers or online platforms for workshops on mindfulness. Workshops often provide practical guidance and opportunities for discussion.

# Chapter 5

## "Crafting a Joyful Life"

As the renowned author and humanitarian, Albert Schweitzer, once remarked, "Success is not the key to happiness. Happiness is the key to success. If you love what you are doing, you will be successful."

This nicely encapsulates the essence of a joyful life—where happiness becomes the driving force and success is a natural byproduct of a fulfilled existence. Having a joyful life goes beyond mere moments of fleeting pleasure; it involves cultivating a deep and abiding sense of contentment, purpose and connection. Healthy habits play a pivotal role in this equation, serving as the foundational bricks that construct the edifice of a joyful life. These habits, whether they involve mindfulness practices, positive relationships, self-care or continuous learning, contribute to a holistic well-being that not only enhances the quality of life but also sets the stage for meaningful success. The pursuit of joy is a lifelong journey and within the framework of healthy habits, people find the tools to navigate this path, creating a harmonious and joyous existence.

# The Happiness Equation:

Neil Pasricha, a Canadian author, speaker and advocate for positivity, is known for his work on happiness and well-being. In his book "The Happiness Equation," Pasricha proposes a simplified formula to represent the factors influencing happiness. While not a literal mathematical equation, it serves as a framework for understanding the elements that contribute to a more joyful life. It is expressed as:

$$H=S+C+V$$

**H - Happiness:** It represents the overall level of happiness or well-being.

**S - Set Point**: Pasricha suggests that a significant portion of happiness is predetermined by genetics and personality traits, representing a "set point." However, he notes that this set point is not fixed and people can influence it through intentional efforts.

**C - Conditions of Living**: Conditions mean the external factors such as income, job and living situation. Pasricha emphasizes that while these factors contribute to happiness, they are not the sole determinants. He encourages people to focus on factors within their control and not solely rely on external circumstances for happiness.

**V - Voluntary Choices:** Voluntary choices represent the intentional actions and decisions people make in their daily lives. Pasricha highlights that these choices, encompassing habits, relationships and activities, have a significant effect on overall happiness. By making positive choices, people can actively enhance their well-being.

Pasricha's Happiness Equation underlines the importance of personal agency and the power of intentional choices in influencing happiness. While external conditions and genetic factors play a role, people have the capacity to shape their well-being through mindful decisions and positive habits. The equation serves as a reminder that happiness is not solely determined by external circumstances but is also influenced by the choices one makes in navigating life.

The voluntary choices (V) in the equation plays attention on the significance of intentional actions and decisions in shaping happiness. Positive habit formation directly aligns with these voluntary choices, offering a practical means for people to enhance their well-being and improve the overall quality of life.

# Building a Supportive Environment:

Social connections form a harmonious melody that profoundly influences our happiness. The bonds we cultivate, the relationships we nurture and the communities we engage with are integral threads in the fabric of well-being. Understanding the profound effect of social connections allows us to create a supportive environment that encourages positive habits and healthy living.

Social connections are not mere accessories to life; they are fundamental pillars of our happiness. Research consistently shows that strong social ties are linked to increased happiness, reduced stress and a greater sense of purpose. Whether it is family, friends or a broader community, our connections play a pivotal role in shaping our emotional landscape.

### Creating a Supportive Environment:

There are several ways to develop a healthy and positive influence around you. Here are some useful strategies that you can employ:

Join clubs, classes or groups that align with your interests. Shared activities provide a natural environment for positive habit reinforcement. While you socialize make sure to draw clear boundaries to avoid unnecessary emotional turmoil. It is crucial to create accountability with friends or family members for your wellness goals and create a supportive framework for growth.

You can also share your healthy eating habits with your support group by preparing and enjoying nutritious meals with others. Another great way to bond with your people is to turn physical activity into a social affair by joining fitness classes or walking groups. The shared experience makes it enjoyable and sustainable.

It is imperative to keep the communication honest and open while you develop meaningful connection. By truly hearing and understanding each other you can foster a deeper connection and contribute to developing a positive social environment. You need to think about open dialogue, expressing thoughts and feelings honestly while creating a space for others to do the same.

While communication with others, it is best to acknowledge and celebrate each other's successes, no matter how small. Positive reinforcement encourages the continuation of healthy habits. Cultivate friendships that uplift and support your well-being. Choose connections that align with your values and contribute positively to your life. Prioritise meaningful connections rather than the quantity of relationships. Regularly express gratitude for the positive effect your social connections have on your life. Practice being fully present during social interactions, fostering genuine connections.

# Overcoming Obstacles and Sustaining Change:

Life's twists and turns may throw obstacles our way, testing our commitment to positive habits. However, resilience, perseverance and strategic navigation can empower us to overcome these challenges. Let's explore strategies to deal with the inevitable hurdles on our path to sustained happiness.

## Mindful Anticipation

Take a moment to identify potential obstacles that may arise in your pursuit of positive habits and a healthy lifestyle. Reflect on previous attempts and think about the challenges that may have derailed your progress.

## Resilience Practices

Embrace mindfulness practices to stay present in the face of challenges. Mindfulness fosters resilience by helping you navigate difficulties with a calm and focused mindset. Instead of viewing setbacks as failures, see them as opportunities for growth. Extract lessons from challenges to enhance your resilience.

**SMART "Specific, Measurable, Achievable, Relevant, Time-bound" Goals**: Set goals that adhere to the SMART criteria. This ensures that your objectives are realistic and manageable, minimizing the likelihood of becoming overwhelmed.

### Flexible Mindset

Life is dynamic and circumstances may shift. Develop a flexible mindset that allows you to adapt your habits to evolving situations. If a particular habit becomes challenging due to changes, think about making small adjustments rather than abandoning it entirely.

### Kindness Toward Yourself

Be gentle with yourself when facing challenges. Treat yourself with the same kindness you would offer to a friend encountering difficulties. Acknowledge and celebrate small victories. Recognizing your achievements, no matter how modest, boosts motivation.

### Continuous Reflection

Periodically reflect on your journey. Assess what's working well and what might need adjustment. If certain strategies prove ineffective, be open to adjusting your approach. Adaptability is key to long-term success.

If challenges persist, think about seeking guidance from professionals such as psychologists, nutritionists or fitness trainers. Their expertise can provide tailored strategies.

## Effective Time Management:

Time management expert, Stephen Covey, recommends prioritizing tasks based on urgency and importance. Set clear boundaries to avoid overcommitting and focus on what truly matters. Overcoming procrastination and staying focused requires a combination of self-awareness, effective habits and strategies. Here are some tips to help you avoid procrastination and stay focused throughout the day:

- **Create Clear Objectives:** Clearly articulating both short-term and long-term goals provides a profound sense of purpose and a well-defined path forward.

- **Deconstruct Tasks into Manageable Segments:** Rather than being overwhelmed by large tasks, fragment them into smaller, more achievable steps. Focus on completing one step at a time to avoid procrastination and maintain momentum.

- **Prioritise Effectively**: Recognize and prioritise tasks based on their urgency and significance. Addressing high-priority tasks first ensures the completion of critical work before delving into less pressing matters.

- **Craft a Daily Action Plan**: Develop a to-do list for the day, preferably the evening before. Organize tasks by priority, and experience a visual sense of accomplishment as you check off completed items.

- **Implement Time Blocking:** Assign specific time blocks for distinct tasks to prevent multitasking. This approach fosters concentrated efforts on one task at a time, enhancing overall efficiency.

- **Set Achievable Deadlines**: Attribute realistic deadlines to tasks to instill a sense of urgency. This practice curbs procrastination and maintains focus on completing tasks within a reasonable timeframe.

- **Minimize Distractions:** Identify and reduce potential disruptions in your workspace. Turning off unnecessary notifications, closing irrelevant tabs or apps, and cultivating a clutter-free environment contribute to sustained focus.

- **Incorporate Breaks**: Acknowledge the importance of breaks in sustaining concentration. Employ techniques such as the Pomodoro Technique, involving focused work intervals followed by short breaks, to optimize productivity.

- **Develop a Morning Ritual**: Initiate your day with a consistent morning routine to foster a positive atmosphere and instill a sense of structure from the outset.

- **Embrace Flexibility and Adaptability**: Cultivate a mindset of flexibility, readily adjusting your schedule when unexpected challenges arise. Being adaptable ensures you can navigate unforeseen circumstances and recalibrate your plan as necessary.

## Tracking Your Progress and Adjust Habits:

A quote I used early was by the esteemed author and motivational speaker Jim Rohn, who said, "Motivation is what gets you started. Habit is what keeps you going." This encapsulates the essence of habit development—initiating positive changes is crucial, but equally vital is the ongoing process of monitoring, adapting and learning. Developing good habits lays the foundation for personal growth, but the true power lies in the consistent evaluation and adjustment of these habits. Tracking habits provides a window into progress, enabling people to assess their efficacy and make informed decisions. Moreover, the ability to adapt and learn new habits, when necessary, ensures flexibility and continual improvement on the path toward personal development and success. The journey from habit formation to sustained growth is a dynamic process, requiring not just initiation but a commitment to ongoing refinement and evolution.

***Select Monitoring Tools***: Choose tools that suit the habits you are monitoring. For an exercise log, fitness apps, journals or specialized trackers can be useful. Ensure the tools are user-friendly and align with your preferences. Say if you are monitoring your exercise habits, you might choose a fitness app like MyFitnessPal to log your workouts, track your progress and set exercise goals. The app provides a user-friendly interface and allows you to customize your tracking based on your preferred exercises and fitness metrics.

***Develop Baseline Metrics:*** Determine baseline metrics for each habit. For exercise, this could include the type of workout, duration, intensity and frequency. Understanding where you currently stand provides a reference point for progress.

***Create a Habit Tracking System***: Develop a habit-tracking system using a daily journal dedicated to your exercise routine. Each day, record the exercises you performed, the duration and any notes about how you felt during the workout. Alternatively, use a specialized habit-tracking app that provides reminders and a seamless interface for

*Set Realistic Targets*: Develop realistic targets for each habit. If you are tracking exercise, set achievable goals for the number of workouts per week or specific fitness milestones. Realistic targets help maintain motivation. If your goal is to increase your exercise habits, set a realistic target such as working out three times a week for 30 minutes each session. Realistic targets prevent burnout and ensure that your goals are attainable, fostering a sense of accomplishment.

*Record Daily Progress*: Consistently record your daily progress. In the case of an exercise log, log the type of exercise, duration and any other relevant details. Be honest in your entries, noting both successes and challenges. If you completed a 30-minute jog, note the distance covered and any specific achievements or challenges. Honesty in your entries allows for accurate self-assessment.

*Use Visual Representations*: Utilize visual cues to make tracking more engaging. Charts, graphs or color-coded systems can provide a quick visual summary of your progress. This visual representation makes it easier to identify patterns and trends. Create visual representations of your exercise habits, such as a line graph showcasing your weekly workout duration. Color-code different types of exercises for a quick overview. Visual cues make it easy to identify trends and areas for improvement.

*Schedule Regular Reviews:* Set aside time regularly to review your habit-tracking data. Weekly or monthly reviews allow you to assess overall progress, identify areas for improvement and make informed decisions for the future. Set aside time each Sunday evening for a weekly review. Evaluate your exercise data, looking for patterns in your routine and identifying any deviations from your goals. Regular reviews provide insights into your progress.

*Reflect on Effect:* Think about the effect of your habits on your work and personal life. Evaluate whether the habits are positively influencing your goals and well-being. If adjustments are needed, make them based on this reflection. Reflect on how your exercise habits effect your overall well-being. If you notice increased energy levels or improved mood on workout days, acknowledge these positive effects. If certain habits are causing stress, think about adjustments.

*Adapt and Adjust*: Be flexible in adapting your habits as needed. If certain exercises or routines are not delivering the desired results, be open to trying new approaches. Adjustments should be informed by your monitoring data. Be open to adapting your exercise routines based on your monitoring data. If you observe that a particular type of workout is not yielding desired results, try incorporating new exercises or adjusting intensity levels.

***Celebrate Milestones***: Celebrate achievements and milestones in your habit-tracking journey. Recognize and reward yourself for reaching specific goals. Positive reinforcement enhances motivation. Rewards could include a relaxing day off or treating yourself to a healthy, enjoyable activity.

***Integrate Learnings into Goals:*** When setting new goals, use insights from your habit-tracking experience. Align your goals with the habits that contribute most to your overall well-being and success. When setting new goals, integrate insights from your habit-tracking experience. If you have identified that morning workouts are more sustainable for you, align your goals with this preference to enhance adherence.

***Stay Consistent and Patient***: Even on days when progress is slow or you face setbacks, stay committed to your exercise routine. Recognize that building habits takes time and be patient with yourself throughout the journey. Consistency is key to long-term success.

# Chapter 6

# The Road to Lasting Happiness

So, what have we learned so far? In the quest for enduring happiness, we must step on a journey paved with intentional choices and mindful living. The road to lasting happiness is not a fleeting sprint but a steady, purposeful walk guided by the incorporation of healthy habits into our daily lives. Happiness, often elusive in the fast-paced world we navigate, is not an external pursuit but an internal state of being. Building a foundation for lasting joy requires a holistic approach that considers both physical and emotional well-being. In this chapter, we delve into the transformative power of cultivating healthy habits.

**The Power of Mindfulness**

At the heart of sustained happiness is the practice of mindfulness—a state of non-judgmental awareness of the present moment. Engaging in mindfulness techniques, such as meditation or simply paying attention to your surroundings, allows you to detach from the chaos the past and the uncertainty of the future. For example, taking a few minutes each day to practice mindful breathing or appreciating the colors and textures during a daily walk can significantly contribute to a more content and fulfilled life.

Start incorporating mindfulness in your daily routine, whether through meditation, deep-breathing exercises or simply paying attention to the sensations around you. As you cultivate this awareness, you will find that the noise of life gradually diminishes, making space for a more profound and enduring happiness.

**Nourishment for the Soul and Body:**
Viewing a healthy diet as nourishment for both the body and soul emphasizes the holistic connection between nutrition and well-being. Treating food choices as an investment in personal health encourages people to opt for a balanced and nutrient-rich diet. For instance, savoring a home-cooked meal made with fresh ingredients not only provides physical nourishment but also contributes to a positive and grateful mindset.

A healthy diet is not only fuel for the body but also a source of vitality for the soul. Think about your food choices as a direct investment in your well-being. Opt for a balanced diet rich in nutrients and savor each bite with gratitude. A well-nourished body is better equipped to manage the physical and emotional challenges that life throws our way.

**The Joy of Movement:**

Regular physical activity is not just about fitness; it is a pathway to happiness. Exercise, whether in the form of a brisk walk, a dance session or a yoga practice, releases endorphins that act as natural mood lifters. For example, engaging in a favorite sport or dance routine provides both physical well-being and emotional balance. Recognizing and finding joy in movement creates a positive feedback loop between the body and mind, contributing to overall happiness.

An active lifestyle is a gateway to happiness. Regular exercise not only enhances physical health but also releases endorphins—the body's natural mood lifters. Find joy in movement, be it through a brisk walk, a dance session or a yoga practice. Physical well-being and emotional balance are intricately linked and an active lifestyle provides the synergy needed for lasting happiness.

**Sustaining Happiness Through Practice:**

The key to lasting happiness lies in the consistency of healthy habits. Rather than viewing these practices as fleeting resolutions, consider them enduring habits that shape your overall well-being over time. Every day offers an opportunity to reaffirm your commitment to happiness through mindfulness, nourishment and movement.

As you begin your life altering experience, remember that the key to lasting happiness lies in consistency. These healthy habits are not mere fleeting resolutions but enduring practices that, over time, shape your overall well-being. See each day as an opportunity to reaffirm your commitment to happiness through mindfulness, nourishment and movement.

# Conclusion

Big, heartfelt thanks for jumping into this adventure with me. Whether you snagged this book or hit the download button, your commitment to a happier, healthier life is seriously impressive. I am genuinely grateful to be a part of your journey. Now that we have wrapped up, I hope you are feeling all pumped up and ready to rock those habits for a lifetime. The real magic, my friend, is when you take what you have soaked in here and put it into action. Armed with a fresh perspective, you are the architect of a life filled with genuine well-being.

Your support is like a rocket fuel for me! If you loved the book, how about taking a sec to share the love on Amazon? Your thoughts not only give me a boost but also help other folks discover the transformation waiting within these pages. Wishing you a future packed with lasting happiness, vibrant health and habits that kickstart your dreams. May your days be filled with joy, purpose and the kind of fulfillment that comes from living your best life.

A massive thank you and I wish you the best of luck with your life-long journey into a happier and healthy life.

Much Love,

Jack

# References:

Craft, L. L., & Perna, F. M. (2004). The benefits of exercise for the clinically depressed. *The Primary Care Companion for CNS Disorders*, *6*(3). https://doi.org/10.4088/pcc.v06n0301

Duhigg, C. (2012). *The power of habit: why we do what we do in life and business*. https://ci.nii.ac.jp/ncid/BB17363429

Hanh, T. N., Warren, M. R., & Vo, D. M. (1991). *The miracle of mindfulness: a manual on meditation.* http://ci.nii.ac.jp/ncid/BA45111697

Kabat-Zinn, J. (2003). Mindfulness-based interventions in context: Past, present, and future. *Clinical Psychology-science and Practice*, *10*(2), 144–156. https://doi.org/10.1093/clipsy.bpg016

Kabat-Zinn, J. (2005). *Wherever you go, there you are: Mindfulness meditation in everyday life.* http://ci.nii.ac.jp/ncid/BA23570260

Pennebaker, J. W., & Francis, M. E. (1996). Cognitive, emotional, and language processes in disclosure. Cognition & emotion, 10(6), 601-626.

Pasricha, N. (2017). *The happiness equation: Want Nothing + Do Anything = Have Everything.* Random House.

Ratey, J. J., & Hagerman, E. (2008). *SPARK: the revolutionary new science of exercise and the brain.* http://ci.nii.ac.jp/ncid/BA9124379X

Tolle, E. (1997). *The Power of Now: A Guide to Spiritual Enlightenment.* http://ci.nii.ac.jp/ncid/BA56671795

Printed in Great Britain
by Amazon

40592425R00056